Christmas Memories

Joy To The World

It Came Upon a Midnight Clear

O Come, O Come, Emmanuel

Hark! The Herald Angels Sing

O Holy Night

O Come, All Ye Faithful

O Little Town of Bethlehem

Silent Night

The Twelve Days of Christmas

Jingle Bells

Auld Lang Syne

Christmas at Nana's

Christmas Cheese Ball

(2) packages of Philadelphia Cream Cheese (softened)
(1) small onion - grated
(1) teaspoon Lawrey's Seasoned Salt
     paprika (for garnish)
(2) bayberry candles and a sprig of holly.
(1) box of Ritz Crackers

Preparation may commence on December 23, not before!
In a medium mixing bowel, soften the cream cheese to room temperature.
When the cheese is soft, grate one small onion.
    Note: Aunt Jo refers to this as "destroying the onion"
Put onion, onion juice, and (1) teaspoon of seasoned salt into softened mixture.
Thoroughly mix all the ingredients until well blended.
Shape into a ball and wrap in plastic wrap. Place in the refrigerator.

December 24.
Around 7:00pm take the cheese ball out and remove the plastic wrap.
Put the cheese ball on your best holiday plate, sprinkle with paprika and
garnish with a sprig of holly on top.
Surround the plate with plenty of Ritz crackers.

Place it next to the family Bible opened and marked with a red ribbon to the
book of Luke. On either side of the table, light two Bayberry candles.
(It should also be noted that bayberry candles were only used at Christmas.)
Make sure everyone has knife and stand back. The cheese ball will magically
disappear before your eyes.

As the cheese ball is being devoured, put on the "Christmas Memories" CD
and sing-along with these great holiday songs.

At around 10:00pm get the family together and head off to the Midnight Candle
Light Service. When you get home, open only one present and get some sleep
for the next days' activities. For many, many years this was the yearly routine
at our home. I hope you also will enjoy the Holiday and make some happy
memories for you and your family.

               Dennis McCorkle and the staff at Music Minus One

1203

Contents

C BOOK - TREBLE CLEF .... Voice, Guitar, Keyboards, Flute, Oboe, Violin, Recorder

C BOOK - BASS CLEF . Trombone, Bassoon, Violoncello, Tuba, Double Bass, Baritone Horn

B♭ BOOK .... Trumpet, Tenor Saxophone, Clarinet, Soprano Saxophone

E♭ BOOK .... Alto Saxophone, Baritone Saxophone

F BOOK .... French Horn, English Horn

ISBN 1-59615-218-4

Joy To The World

Program 1 & 12
C Instrument

Words by Isaac Watts, ca.1719
Music arranged by Lowell Mason from the works of George F. Handel

It Came Upon The Midnight Clear

Program 2 & 13
C Instrument

Words by Edmund Hamilton Sears, ca.1846
Music by Richard Storrs Willis, ca.1850

O Come, O Come, Emmanuel

Program 3 and 14
C Instrument

13th Century Plainsong, adapted in 1854 by Thomas Helmore
Words translated by John S. Neale and Henry S. Coffin

Hark the Herald Angels Sing

Program 4 & 15
C Instrument

Words by Charles Wesley, ca.1739
Music by Felix Mendelssohn, ca.1840

O Holy Night

Program 5 & 16
C Instrument

English Words by J.S. Dwight
Music by Adolphe Adam

O Come, All Ye Faithful

Program 6 & 17
C Instrument

Words and Music by John F. Wade, ca.1751
Translated into English by Frederick Oakley

O Little Town of Bethlehem

Program 7 & 18
C Instrument

Words by Phillips Brooks, ca.1867
Music by Lewis H. Redner, ca.1868

Silent Night

12

Program 8 & 19
C Instrument

Words by Jospeh Mohr, ca.1818
Music by Franz Grüeber, ca.1818

The Twelve Days of Christmas

Program 9 & 20
C Instrument

Traditional

On the first day of Christ-mas, my true love gave to me: A par-tridge in a pear tree.

2. On the sec-ond day of Christ-mas, my
3. On the third day of Christ-mas, my
4. On the fourth day of Christ-mas, my

Repeat as needed

D.S. for verses 3 - 4

true love sent to me: Two tur-tle doves,
true love sent to me: Three French hens,
true love sent to me: Four call-ing birds,

And a par-tridge in a pear tree.

On the fifth day of Christ-mas, my true love sent to me: Five gold

rings. Four call-ing birds, Three French hens, Two tur-tle doves, And a

par-tridge in a pear tree.

Fine

6. On the sixth day of Christ-mas, my true love sent to me:
7. On the sev-enth day of Christ-mas, my true love sent to me:
8. On the eighth day of Christ-mas, my true love sent to me:
9. On the ninth day of Christ-mas, my true love sent to me:
10. On the tenth day of Christ-mas, my true love sent to me:
11. On the 'lev-enth day of Christ-mas, my true love sent to me:
12. On the twelfth day of Christ-mas, my true love sent to me:

To ⊕ for verses 7 - 12

Six geese a-lay-ing.
Sev-en swans a-swim-ing.
Eight maids a-milk-ing.
Nine la-dies danc-ing.
Ten lords a-leap-ing.
'Lev-en pi-pers pip-ing.
Twelve drum-mers drum-ing.

Five gold rings!

To Fine after (12)

Jingle Bells

Program 10 & 21
C Instrument

Words and Music by
J. Pierpont

Auld Lang Syne

Program 11 & 22
C Instrument

Traditional

16

Joy To The World

Program 1 & 12
C Instrument

Words by Isaac Watts, ca.1719
Music arranged by Lowell Mason from the works of George F. Handel

It Came Upon The Midnight Clear

Program 2 & 13
C Instrument

Words by Edmund Hamilton Sears, ca.1846
Music by Richard Storrs Willis, ca.1850

O Come, O Come, Emmanuel

Program 3 and 14
C Instrument

13th Century Plainsong, adapted in 1854 by Thomas Helmore
Words translated by John S. Neale and Henry S. Coffin

(Last time)

Hark the Herald Angels Sing

Program 4 & 15
C Instrument

Words by Charles Wesley, ca.1739
Music by Felix Mendelssohn, ca.1840

O Holy Night

Program 5 & 16
C Instrument

English Words by J.S. Dwight
Music by Adolphe Adam

O Come, All Ye Faithful

Program 6 & 17
C Instrument

Words and Music by John F. Wade, ca.1751
Translated into English by Frederick Oakley

O Little Town of Bethlehem

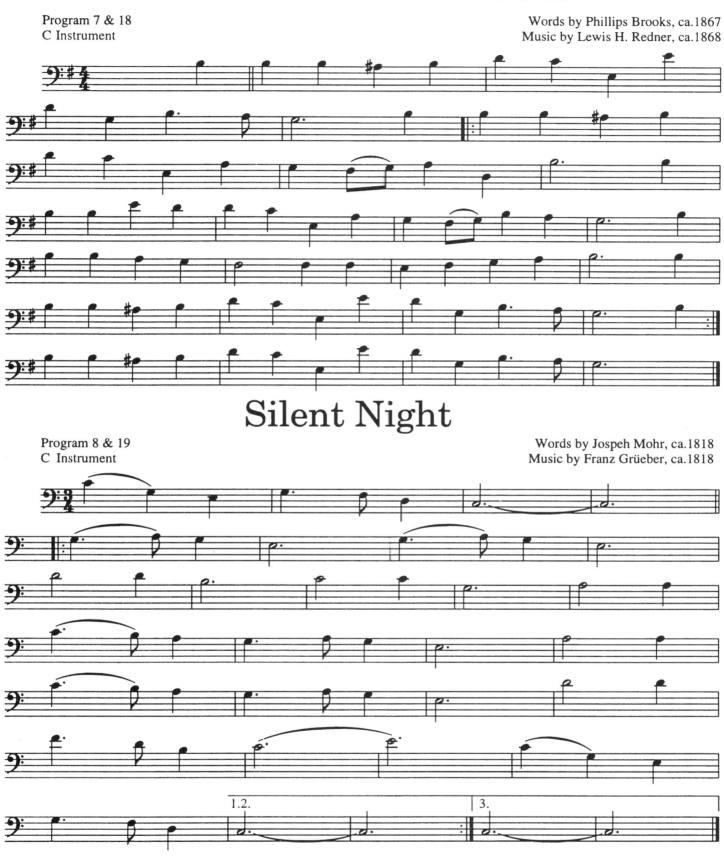

Program 7 & 18
C Instrument

Words by Phillips Brooks, ca.1867
Music by Lewis H. Redner, ca.1868

Silent Night

Program 8 & 19
C Instrument

Words by Jospeh Mohr, ca.1818
Music by Franz Grüeber, ca.1818

The Twelve Days of Christmas

Program 9 & 20
C Instrument

Traditional

Jingle Bells

Program 10 & 21
C Instrument

Words and Music by
J. Pierpont

Auld Lang Syne

Program 11 & 22
C Instrument

Traditional

Joy To The World

Program 1 & 12
Bb Instrument

Words by Isaac Watts, ca.1719
Music arranged by Lowell Mason from the works of George F. Handel

It Came Upon The Midnight Clear

Program 2 & 13
Bb Instrument

Words by Edmund Hamilton Sears, ca.1846
Music by Richard Storrs Willis, ca.1850

O Come, O Come, Emmanuel

23

Program 3 and 14
Bb Instrument

13th Century Plainsong, adapted in 1854 by Thomas Helmore
Words translated by John S. Neale and Henry S. Coffin

(Last time)

Hark the Herald Angels Sing

Program 4 & 15
Bb Instrument

Words by Charles Wesley, ca.1739
Music by Felix Mendelssohn, ca.1840

O Holy Night

Program 5 & 16
Bb Instrument

English Words by J.S. Dwight
Music by Adolphe Adam

O Come, All Ye Faithful

Program 6 & 17
Bb Instrument

Words and Music by John F. Wade, ca.1751
Translated into English by Frederick Oakley

O Little Town of Bethlehem

Program 7 & 18
Bb Instrument

Words by Phillips Brooks, ca.1867
Music by Lewis H. Redner, ca.1868

Repeat 3X

Silent Night

Program 8 & 19
Bb Instrument

Words by Jospeh Mohr, ca.1818
Music by Franz Grüeber, ca.1818

The Twelve Days of Christmas

Program 9 & 20
Bb Instrument

Traditional

On the first day of Christ-mas, my true love gave to me: A par-tridge in a pear tree.

{ 2. On the sec-ond day of Christ-mas, my
3. On the third day of Christ-mas, my
4. On the fourth day of Christ-mas, my

Repeat as needed

D.S. for verses 3 - 4

true love sent to me: Two tur-tle doves,
true love sent to me: Three French hens, } And a par-tridge in a pear tree.
true love sent to me: Four call-ing birds,

On the fifth day of Christ-mas, my true love sent to me: Five gold _____

rings. Four _ call-ing birds, Three French hens, Two _ tur-tle doves, And a

par-tridge in a pear tree.

Fine

6. On the sixth _ day of Christ-mas, my true love sent to me:
7. On the sev-enth day of Christ-mas, my true love sent to me:
8. On the eighth day of Christ-mas, my true love sent to me:
9. On the ninth _ day of Christ-mas, my true love sent to me:
10. On the tenth _ day of Christ-mas, my true love sent to me:
11. On the 'lev-enth day of Christ-mas, my true love sent to me:
12. On the twelfth _ day of Christ-mas, my true love sent to me:

To ⊕ for verses 7 - 12

Six _____ geese a - lay - ing.
Sev - en swans a - swim-ing.
Eight maids a - milk-ing.
Nine la - dies danc-ing.   Five gold _____ rings!
Ten lords a - leap-ing.
'Lev - en pi - pers pip - ing.
Twelve drum - mers drum-ing.

To Fine after (12)

Jingle Bells

Program 10 & 21
Bb Instrument

Words and Music by
J. Pierpont

Auld Lang Syne

Program 11 & 22
Bb Instrument

Traditional

Joy To The World

Program 1 & 12
Eb Instrument

Words by Isaac Watts, ca.1719
Music arranged by Lowell Mason from the works of George F. Handel

It Came Upon The Midnight Clear

Program 2 & 13
Eb Instrument

Words by Edmund Hamilton Sears, ca.1846
Music by Richard Storrs Willis, ca.1850

O Come, O Come, Emmanuel

Program 3 and 14
Eb Instrument

13th Century Plainsong, adapted in 1854 by Thomas Helmore
Words translated by John S. Neale and Henry S. Coffin

Hark the Herald Angels Sing

Program 4 & 15
Eb Instrument

Words by Charles Wesley, ca.1739
Music by Felix Mendelssohn, ca.1840

(Last time)

O Holy Night

Program 5 & 16
Eb Instrument

English Words by J.S. Dwight
Music by Adolphe Adam

O Come, All Ye Faithful

Program 6 & 17
Eb Instrument

Words and Music by John F. Wade, ca.1751
Translated into English by Frederick Oakley

O Little Town of Bethlehem

Program 7 & 18
Eb Instrument

Words by Phillips Brooks, ca.1867
Music by Lewis H. Redner, ca.1868

Repeat 3X

Silent Night

Program 8 & 19
Eb Instrument

Words by Jospeh Mohr, ca.1818
Music by Franz Grüeber, ca.1818

1.2.   3.

The Twelve Days of Christmas

Program 9 & 20
Eb Instrument

Traditional

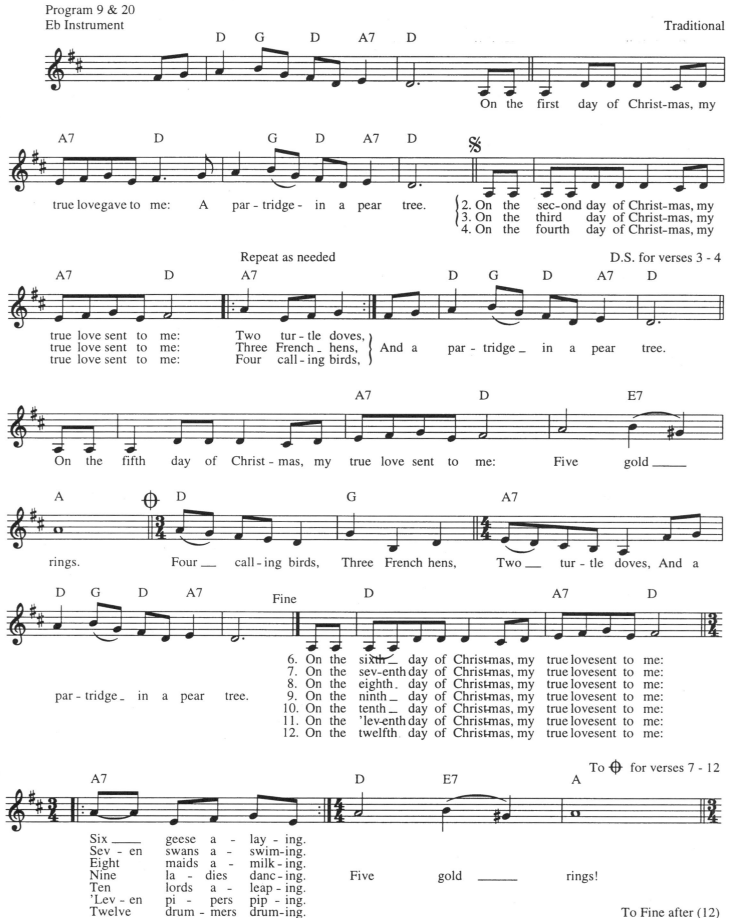

On the first day of Christ-mas, my
true love gave to me: A par-tridge in a pear tree.

{ 2. On the sec-ond day of Christ-mas, my
{ 3. On the third day of Christ-mas, my
{ 4. On the fourth day of Christ-mas, my

Repeat as needed

D.S. for verses 3 - 4

true love sent to me: Two tur-tle doves,
true love sent to me: Three French hens,   } And a par-tridge in a pear tree.
true love sent to me: Four call-ing birds, }

On the fifth day of Christ-mas, my true love sent to me: Five gold _____

rings. Four _ call-ing birds, Three French hens, Two _ tur-tle doves, And a

Fine

par-tridge _ in a pear tree.

6. On the sixth _ day of Christ-mas, my true love sent to me:
7. On the sev-enth day of Christ-mas, my true love sent to me:
8. On the eighth _ day of Christ-mas, my true love sent to me:
9. On the ninth _ day of Christ-mas, my true love sent to me:
10. On the tenth _ day of Christ-mas, my true love sent to me:
11. On the 'lev-enth day of Christ-mas, my true love sent to me:
12. On the twelfth _ day of Christ-mas, my true love sent to me:

To ⊕ for verses 7 - 12

Six _____ geese a - lay - ing.
Sev - en swans a - swim-ing.
Eight maids a - milk-ing.
Nine la - dies danc-ing.   Five gold _____ rings!
Ten lords a - leap-ing.
'Lev - en pi - pers pip-ing.
Twelve drum - mers drum-ing.

To Fine after (12)

Jingle Bells

Program 10 & 21
Eb Instrument

Words and Music by
J. Pierpont

Auld Lang Syne

Program 11 & 22
Eb Instrument

Traditional

Joy To The World

Program 1 & 12
F Instrument

Words by Isaac Watts, ca.1719
Music arranged by Lowell Mason from the works of George F. Handel

It Came Upon The Midnight Clear

Program 2 & 13
F Instrument

Words by Edmund Hamilton Sears, ca.1846
Music by Richard Storrs Willis, ca.1850

O Come, O Come, Emmanuel

Program 3 and 14
F Instrument

13th Century Plainsong, adapted in 1854 by Thomas Helmore
Words translated by John S. Neale and Henry S. Coffin

(Last time)

Hark the Herald Angels Sing

Program 4 & 15
F Instrument

Words by Charles Wesley, ca.1739
Music by Felix Mendelssohn, ca.1840

O Holy Night

Program 5 & 16
F Instrument

English Words by J.S. Dwight
Music by Adolphe Adam

O Come, All Ye Faithful

Program 6 & 17
F Instrument

Words and Music by John F. Wade, ca.1751
Translated into English by Frederick Oakley

O Little Town of Bethlehem

Program 7 & 18
F Instrument

Words by Phillips Brooks, ca.1867
Music by Lewis H. Redner, ca.1868

Silent Night

Program 8 & 19
F Instrument

Words by Jospeh Mohr, ca.1818
Music by Franz Grüeber, ca.1818

The Twelve Days of Christmas

Program 9 & 20
F Instrument

Traditional

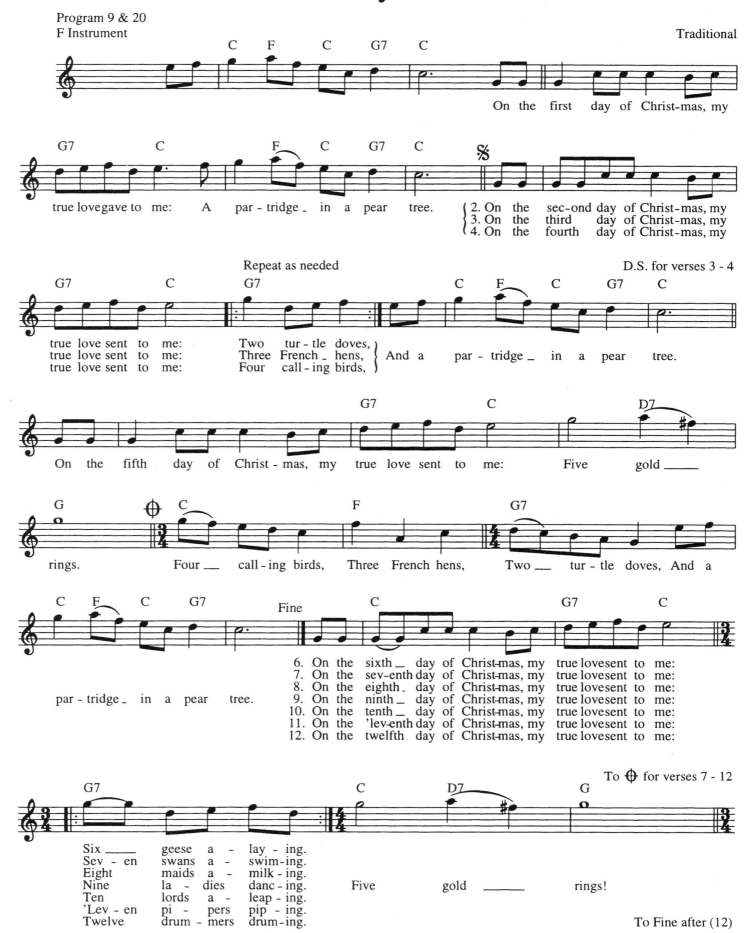

On the first day of Christ-mas, my true lovegave to me: A par-tridge in a pear tree.

2. On the sec-ond day of Christ-mas, my
3. On the third day of Christ-mas, my
4. On the fourth day of Christ-mas, my

Repeat as needed

D.S. for verses 3 - 4

true love sent to me: Two tur-tle doves,
true love sent to me: Three French hens,
true love sent to me: Four call-ing birds,

And a par-tridge in a pear tree.

On the fifth day of Christ-mas, my true love sent to me: Five gold _____ rings.

Four _ call-ing birds, Three French hens, Two _ tur-tle doves, And a par-tridge _ in a pear tree.

Fine

6. On the sixth _ day of Christ-mas, my true lovesent to me:
7. On the sev-enth day of Christ-mas, my true lovesent to me:
8. On the eighth . day of Christ-mas, my true lovesent to me:
9. On the ninth _ day of Christ-mas, my true lovesent to me:
10. On the tenth _ day of Christ-mas, my true lovesent to me:
11. On the 'lev-enth day of Christ-mas, my true lovesent to me:
12. On the twelfth . day of Christ-mas, my true lovesent to me:

To ✪ for verses 7 - 12

Six _____ geese a - lay - ing.
Sev - en swans a - swim-ing.
Eight maids a - milk - ing.
Nine la - dies danc - ing.
Ten lords a - leap - ing.
'Lev - en pi - pers pip - ing.
Twelve drum - mers drum-ing.

Five gold _____ rings!

To Fine after (12)

Jingle Bells

Program 10 & 21
F Instrument

Words and Music by
J. Pierpont

Auld Lang Syne

Program 11 & 22
F Instrument

Traditional

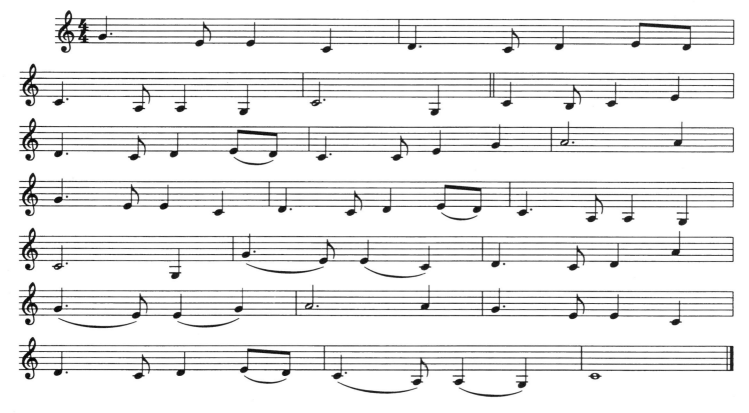

MUSIC MINUS ONE
50 Executive Boulevard
Elmsford, New York 10523-1325
1.800.669.7464 (U.S.)/914.592.1188 (International)

www.musicminusone.com
e-mail: mmogroup@musicminusone.com